DISPOSSESSED

DISPOSSESSED

Modikwe Dikobe

RAVAN PRESS JOHANNESBURG

Published by Ravan Press (Pty) Ltd
P.O. Box 31134, Braamfontein, 2017

First published 1983

ISBN 086975 143 3

Typesetting: Ginah Dludla
Cover portrait: Mpikayipheli Figlan
Cover design: The Graphic Equalizer
Printed by Blackshaws, Cape Town

CONTENTS

MY UMBILICAL CORD

Here my umbilical cord fell
Fell into this black soil
And washed into Mutshe river
Sixty-five years ago.

I search in the marshes
For my umbilical cord
In the marshes of Mutshe river
In vain.

I am told
Some monster is laying hands
On where my umbilical cord fell
Devastating it into next-to-nothing.

TIME IMMEMORIAL PART 1

On the slope of this mountain
Happily lived my forefathers
    In affluence.
Happily they lived on this mountain.
Festivals, weddings not in want.

Afar field crops, they harvested.
They organised hunting: in letsolo or singles.
Afar field beyond those hills
They herded their cattle
Herdboys moulding cattle,
Hunting games,
Never was there a day of dearth.

Then on an unknown day
Dust rose far-away
As if of a storm; of rain dust;
A driving hurricane.
    'Matabele on warpath,' said the greyheaded.
    'Every man to arms!' commanded the chief.

Man to man they stood on that sad evening,
Blood gushing as from slaughtered ox,
Women on mountain top 'lulling' their men.
Here and there men fell; clutching a spear.
    'Fight to the last man.'

Are my ears deceiving me?
Hearing murmurings below this boulder.
    'You tread on my head.'
Am I crazy, possessed in spirit?
Hearing a low beating drum
Moving to tears —

'Dum, dum, dum.'

Surely Ramabifi you're a living ghost
Badimo hovering within you.
Nay; let me tarry no longer.

TIME IMMEMORIAL PART II

Time is past, fast and swift
Time of cannibals
Time stalking for human flesh
Remembered only by the aged.
On mountain slopes
Unrecorded memory
Marked on rocks
Buried here.
Grandfather
Holding a scimitar
Brave man was he
Slew his foe.

Time immemorial
Incredible murmuring
'You tread on my head'
Broken bowls, pots, copper ornaments
Strewn about
A shadowy figure
Grinding, grinding endlessly.

In a moulded heap
Marked in oblong
Sits she
Hands folded
Amassed around
Is the pride of her household
Equipped
On her journey
To her ancestors.

DISPOSSESSED

I
You were born in affluence
Land as vast as sea
Pegging, pegging each seasonal year
A plot for ploughing
Hundreds of livestock you possessed
Your dwellings a fortress
Your wives as many as your fingers
Each night, a different woman
Not a word of grouse.

Someone arrived
Helmeted he was
Astride a white horse
Attention, he demanded,
    'Get me a fire kindled
    Draw water for me
    Get one of your sons to look after my horse.'
In the open he chose to sleep
A gun by his side.

He was awake earlier than you
Inspecting everything on sight
Casting his face afar
Noting, Noting, Noting
Giving a scornful smile
As he looked at you
Turning his face in satisfaction
Murmuring: 'Blooming Kaffir'.

A year later
He returned
Accompanied by a troop of police

He strode in front on a white horse
   'Get tents ready, boys'.
He commanded his men.
In an hour a town is pitched
A flag hoisted
A bugle sounded
   'Fall in.' He lined up his men
Each a duty: tonight.
Your unlettered brain pronounced
ZARP! 'Mai-is-isi'
Stupid you were
Not to say Zuid-Afrikaanse Polisie.

You were discontinued from trying cases
   'Call a pitso,'
You were ordered
Head tax. Hut tax. Dip tax.
All piled on you
Hard cash. With Queen Victoria's head
A golden sovereign
Minted somewhere you don't know.

I know you're hard put to part with a beast
Each is worth more than a sovereign
They resemble your gods
Only at your funeral
Shall some be slaughtered
Bedding you in cattle pen
A stick in hand.
Squatting. Conscious of duties.
Hover about your kraal
Day and night.

II
You were ordered to call a pitso

6

To Mai-is-isi camp
You were told men are wanted
To dig diamonds out of the earth.
You cannot pay your tax by selling cattle.
Golden sovereign. Queen Victoria's Head.
You marked X against your name
You raised two fingers 'Modimo nthuse — God help
me'.

You bid farewell to your wives
None cried because your custom allows
No crying.
Soldiers to battle.

A long column. Day and night
You walked; tired, fatigued, thirsty, parched throat.
Feet sore. Some could no longer walk
Died. Buried by the wayside
'Lebitla la monna le tseleng — Man's grave is by the
wayside'.

Every night your stick never forgotten
Placed westwards
Path to be followed.

Village, village built as your home
In sight
Happy hearts
Hearing human beings like yourself
Speaking your own dialect
Homes like your woman
'Morena — lord! This is unbelievable
Unbelievable to see women like our own
Where are your men?'
    'Kimilie.'
'How far is that place?'
'Two days two nights from here'.

Pack your box
A roll of material
For your wives
A guinea piece for each
A three-legged pot
To cook on the way
        Farewell!

IV
In your absence:
The Government has impounded some of your cattle;
        Dip taxation
        Tick sickness
        Mouth and foot disease
        Tsetse fly
        And culling
You're poor now

Look around:
        New dwellings
        Your 'fortress' dispersed
        Your junior wife gone.

The shopkeeper wants to see you
        Mealie meal credit
        Clothing material
        Taken by your junior wife.

Your son is gone
        To Johannesburg
        Your seniority is usurped.
Nothing is left. Take another contract.

Very hospitable are these women
Food. Locust nourishment for supper.
    'Spirits of our fathers
    You've travelled along with us.
    No cannibal has eaten us
    Nor a lion.
    Keep evilness away from us.'

Thirty men are sprawled within the enclosure
Soundless sleep
Unfelt in three full moons
Their flesh numbed
Flabby as liver.

No sorcerer will touch you
For you look like witches yourselves
You resemble badikana
You resemble initiation boys
You terrify cats and dogs
You look like the bewitched.

III
You arrive when working conditions are improved
In the past men worked hard
Worked by shoulder
Carrying buckets.
Now it's headgear. Ropes.
Dragging from the bottom
Sebenza, Turn the headgear, Dig.
The boss has made me boss-boy
You, sebenza.
Forget your wife. Make extra money.
You're sexual as your sister.

You're here to save money

To pay poll-tax
Twelve months of contract
Save your money in a syrup tin
Lock your box
Don't visit the native location
Oorlams they are
Forgotten their culture
Their language
'Kaffir' they shall say of you
Real oorlams, bushmen, Rolong, Thlaping, hotten-
tots
A league of Bantu tribes.

You can visit on week-ends
By the roadside, near the diggings
Is a meeting:
'Native Land Act, Pass-laws, Poll-tax.'
You will be urged to join the Native Union
A national organisation
Undoing your way of thinking
Unknotting your tribal affiliation.
But look, don't fall into beer dens
Prostitution is legalized
Legalized by concession
'Don't cohabit in public.'

Spare enough of your sperm
Three wives are not easy to satisfy
Each a night
Two nights to recuperate
But don't hide venereal disease
See a compound doctor
Don't waste your money on herbal medicines.

Your contract is over

LORD ALLEN BARRY

Though your burial place
Is erased
Someone says:
    It's here
Where your pipe smoked out
    Fairland farm.

You're a dreaded memory
To those who laboured
In your lordship
Dreading your sight, your voice
Commanding like a colonel.

You're a memory
Of a pot-belly pipe
Chain-smoking across the plain
On a trotting horse
Chain-smoking.

'Here ends my farm,'
    You exclaimed
'Where my pipe stops smoking.'

Your domain was an estate
A land of survey
British Empire estate
Lord of Wales
You're forgotten.

SKONFAAN

A distilling syndicate
In Sunnyside east of Pretoria
In a bid to compete
Conceived viable idea
For 'Kaffir' trade.

East of Pretoria, Sunnyside,
Yeast, sugar brewed in lukewarm water
A kick-off brand.

In Sunnyside, east of Pretoria,
The distilling company flourished
With the skonfaan brand
The servants were a nuisance
They drank skonfaan in public
And made love in the street.

In Sunnyside, east of Pretoria,
The residents complained:
        'The police must stop this nuisance.'
And in Pienaarsrivier:
        'The state must intervene,'
Demanded a monopoly king.

In Brickor, Sunnyside,
East of Pretoria,
Sprang up another company
In a brickyard
Flooded by labourers.

In a brickyard, east of Pretoria,
Flourished the brickyard syndicate
In groups the customers drank

And made love in the brick ovens.

In Sunnyside, east of Pretoria,
In a brickyard
The brand found its name
        'SKONFAAN'.

BENEVOLENT MASTER

You're not to complain.
For two hundred years
I've borne the burden.
I've baptized you
Given you education
And made you what you are
Today.

I am now leaving you
To my neighbour.
Money, buildings, teachers,
He commands.
But never complain
Of what he gives you.

NGUDULANA

The case is heard in public by an English magistrate.

Ngudulana
You're an Ndebele chief
In Bultfontein, near Rust DeWinter.
    'Kunjalo nkosi.'

You're charged with a very serious crime
Of taking a white woman
To your native school.
    's'Ndebele.'

You shaved her hair
Ochred her head
Paraded her bare-breasted
And caused her private parts
To be mutilated.
    's'Ndebele.'

Your case
Is to be heard by the landdrost
In Nylstroom
    'Skiet hom nou dood.'

BEGGING

Day to day
I walk this route
Knocking door to door
Searching dustbins
For crumbs of bread,
Dogs barking
'Catch him, Spider.'

My feet are swift
Motionless swift
Spider no match
Not when I've snatched
A bottle of wine
From the table.

I would be learning alphabets
Had not fate destined me orphanage
From the day I fell out of my mother's womb
Cursed illegitimate
Scorned by society.

MARABASTAD

I
In Mamelodi, I was told an anecdote
Of a man, a chief, who arrived
In Mamelodi before the Anglo-Boer War
With a group of followers
At the edge of Polokwane.

On a piece of land
West of Mamelodi
He settled near the Tshwane River.

Homage he received
From neighbouring tribes
Black and white
Across the Tshwane River
And named the settlement
    MARABASTAD.

At nagmaal festival
His neighbours
Invited him to witness whiteman's religion
On lull days
Nagmaal was sold in calabashes.

In timitis sold in pafana
In streets sold in bottles
Young and old flocked into timitis
Broke the old rule
Of young and old apart.

Popular he became, chief Maraba
The young ones revolted
    'Ons gaan marabi toe.'

'Devilish,' protested the parents.

II
Famous he became, the chief
Expectation in Johannesburg
In Sophiatown: 'Ons gaan marabi toe.'
In Doornfontein: 'Reya marabing.'
In Prospect Township: 'Siya marabing.'

FUNERAL OF A PATHFINDER

Play the Last Post
Sound it to the heavenly angels
Beloved was he in pathfinding
Along Eloff Street
How the 'Bantus' are coming.

Disgusted did they disapprove
Of the refusal to the World Jamboree
By the stroke of a pen
From the hierarchy of the NAD.

      'Stem met Grobler.'
In wit dorp to permit 'Kaffirs' scouting.

To Steven's Farm echoed in the bush
Kettle drumming of that wonderful boy
In rhyme to marching.

Play the Last Post
Ye pathfinders of Jo'burg
Sound it to the heavens
To angels' trumping melody,
Floating his spirit to God's Kingdom
Forever. Amen.

ROSIE I: BACKYARD BOYFRIEND

Sleep, my dear, you and I
Are forced to sleep
In the backyard room
To serve the needs
Of those empowered by law.

Don't worry, sweetie,
It's only temporary
It's God's bidding
That we suffer
Paying for the mistakes of our forefathers.

In three hundred years
By labouring, humiliation, imprisonment
We're paying
God is listening
With two ears.

On the banks of the Jordan
We pray
Make offerings
Beat drums
Raise dust
Praising Him
Hallelujah, Amen.

God is not a fool
To allow oppressors to oppress
Perpetually
Surely some day
You and I shall raise
A family in better circumstances.

ROSIE II: M'CAPPIES

Daily a column passes my gate
Limping behind M'cappies
Twirling into Twist Street
Like birds in palaver
They assemble.

Nobody dare raise protest
In the name of democracy
Fear grips them
Dumb.

Like a Scottish miner
Peak-capped
M'cappies reigns terror
In the hearts of job-seekers.

Yonder within a hill
A thousand voices sing
For the warmth of Rosie
'Rosie, with whom are
You sleeping tonight?'
Chorus
'On your cosy breast
Rosie will you not lock me out
When I finish my sentence?'

ROSIE III: FADING HOPE

Only a few weeks ago
I was saying God is not a fool
You're now sick
I keep you locked in
For fear of being discovered
Elsewhere, John, something is amiss.

'Maggie, your way of thinking
Is baffling.'

It is caused by uncertainty
In daily life:
Forbearance trodden
Perseverance scorned
Tolerance implied as acquiescing.

ROSIE IV: SLEEEPLESS NIGHTS

There's a rumbling of Kwela-kwelas outside,
Shuffling feet,
Piercing hoarse voices
And rattling doors.
Quick, disguise yourself
As a night soil remover
Nobody dare stop Sampogane.

The lavatory pail
Is full to the brim,
Quick! —
Waste no minute.

ROSIE V: AFTERMATH

You're cold as a refrigerator
Tell me how you fared.

> I counted ten trucks
> Massed.
> Torchlights as of a ghost
> Returning to its grave
> Flashed on every yard.
> I slipped through the cordon
> Splashing the contents.
>
> In a vast yard
> I left the pail on the gate.
>
> Like a night watchman
> I took my position
> A kerrie in hand
> Stopped a policeman,
> 'I am in charge!' I said.

Have a rest, Sweetie,
God is seeing all our sufferings.
A day shall come;
A day of fate.

ROSIE VI: EAR TELEPHONE I

I had thought you would soon recover
But now I hear
There will be a raid tonight.

Two blocks away
Is a big house,
As large as Castle brewery,
Trees as many as in Knysna;
Hide there.

    'Rosie, you're amazing,
    Where did you hear that?'

We women are ear telephones
In the parks we hear news
Of what will take place
Every day.
We exchange ideas
How to treat men,
You, I vowed,
I shall never forsake.

ROSIE VII: EAR TELEPHONE II

Rumour is rife
Of a big police raid tonight
Against backyard lodgers
Against passless blacks.

'Rosie you're amazing.'

We women pass information
We're ear telephones
Alert to what goes around
Advising each other
How to treat our boyfriends
You, I vowed, I shall never forsake.

There's a house away from here
As big as Castle brewery
Go there tonight: pose as a nightwatchman.

ROSIE VIII: NANNIES' PROTEST

Along Jan Smuts Avenue
There's a protest march
Of nannies to the city hall
Singing as they march
        'Morena boloka.'

Behind them are kiddies
Holding their aprons
In support of their action.

The major is called upon
To explain so many arrests
Of peaceful, law-abiding backyard boyfriends.

In the chambers
The mayor and the councillors
Will face a barrage of questions
From white ladies.

They're threatening to unseat him
Unless he stops backyard raids
        'I don't understand, Rosie?'

I am chairlady
Of the Nannies' League.
Someone has left a note
On the kitchen door
Informing me of the protest.

WHISPERING WALLS

Whisper me who's in sympathy
I've had no news
Since I arrived
Snugged safely within your walls
And fed like a pig.

Two hours of sunshine
Is insufficient
Not enough for my lungs' appetite.
Couldn't you allow me
One hour more?
Whilst you're still replenished.

Are tax-payers not complaining —
Their money spent on a parasite
Choosing jail rather than work?

I confide in you
Not to tell anybody
The day that I leave.

SHANTYTOWN REMOVAL

I
I shall never forget that winter morning
A rainy November morning
They dismantled our shantytown
Mindless of sleeping souls
Fast asleep as of anaesthesia.

Unforeseen convoy headlights
Heading to our shantytown
Motionless as of a ghost
Returning to its grave in early morning.

Morena! I thought I was dreaming
As at the bank of the Klip River
Sprawled on the bank; demobbed soldiers
To demob our peaceful camp
In the name of human rights
In the year of allied nations.

O! Merciful Lord
Am I sleeping in the open
As in Lombardy estate
In that year of the King's visit,
Or is it a repetition of demobbed soldiers
On the banks of Canada stream,
Or just a deranged mind?

A stinking lavatory hole there,
A heap of rubbish here,
A stray dog there
It's all that is left.
In twice a big town
Housing a thousand souls

With its own administration.

I, alone, with a wife and a child,
Am left in this ruin
Once, the pride of my administration,
Whipped away are those
Who vowed: 'We shall stand by our leader.'
Left in the mercy of the documents.

II
Powerless, hopeless, I lead nobody
I am unfeathered
Left wingless
        Dumbfounded.
South, west, we are being driven in circles
Spanning in confusion
A mine dump, head-gear, mine column, a lake,
A river bend; seamlessly flowing
Not as I saw it on demobbed day.

KLIP RIVER

Calm your current
We're strangers in this country
Beyond those towers, we come from
Beyond sight of eye.

Be kind to bridge across
We shall daily disturb you
Drawing your water
Passing over you.

We shall sing you
In wedding processions
In festivals
Your rhyme moves our feet
   'Klip river, Klip river,
    Klip river, noka e tletse metsi
    Redikile re tlhagola sekolo 'nkoti'

We're unwanted in this land
Across the rail is an office
Issuing orders
To arrest trespassers.

Albert Street is not a home for the homeless
Thousands seeking accommodation
In yellow record card marked
   'NOT QUALIFIED FOR ACCOMMODATION.'

Drive your current into the Vaal River
Fill it to the brim
Touch the floor swiftly and lightly
Spread your wings over the banks
Silently as calm as a sea.

SHEBEEN QUEEN

Drink, my dear,
This is pure brandy
Brewed in Korea
Bottled in Malay Camp
Delivered by the flying squad.

Don't cough, my dear,
You'll scare the customers.
The ingredients are excellent:
    Methylated spirit, tobacco juice, yeast, marijuana.
And of course a pint of vinegar
For colouring.

A nip is enough
To get you topsyturvy
You won't get bad dreams
Sleep sound as in death
No worry about spananki.

Take a tot, my dear,
To take off babalaz
It's every drinker's complaint
You'll be alright soon.

Wash your face
Here comes Mack
My best customer
Slight off for a few hours.

SOPHIATOWN VOCALIST

Sing brother for living
Job reservation is law
Your job is pick and shovel
Your education does not count
You were taught to understand
Your master's orders.

The streets are dreary without you
You would have already pocketed a shilling
Messengers, loafers around you
Fingers engaged in handbags.

Change your style
Tap dance
Swing your walking stick
Open your mouth wide
African culture has no limit.

Look out for the pick-up van
Get your pass ready
Marshall Square cells are cold
Deep down in a basement
Opposite Maclaren Street.

You're famous, brother,
Your voice is heard
In Chicago, Harlem
And in District Six
But you're still poor.

R G

None shall ever equal R.G.
Owning half of Alexandra Township
'Safe return Mighty Six'
Master of the road
Roaring along Louis Botha
Out-running
      Green's
      Alexandra Limited
      Laub's
      Jackson's.

From Second to Third Avenues
R.G. Proprietary Ltd.,
Rental pouring into leaking pockets
Signing cheques with the power of attorney
Charity at whim.
      'Stop the Rent Board.'
In the confusion
All business stops
Adjourned sine die
A bull in the chinaman's shop.

Honour bestowed upon those
Who in service trusted
Not a sovereign unrecorded
Balance sheet as clean as a sheet
Great man was he — R.G.
In the N.R.C. chambers
Full two hours speech
Without banging.

Mourn Alexandra Township,

Mourn the nation.
In poverty he died
Benevolent, charitable
Signing cheques.

If sincerity is disputable,
Not to R.G.
Poor he died
Proving his sincerity.

MART-ZULU

If it were yesterday
I would venture out after sunset
Plod in the alleys of Alexandra Township
And remind you
That tomorrow
There's a meeting.

You would have had no reason
To complain
Of being disturbed at that hour
Because you, alone,
Raised me.

Years gone by
You trained me verbatim
        'Bhala!'
You ordered me
Word by word —
Would you now curse me as a pest?

How very few know me?
Nurtured by you, a raw Zulu,
On No-man's land
Facing a hail of stones.

You would have been a commander-in-chief
In Cetshwayo's wars
Had you not arrived late.

HUSH MY CHILD

Sleep, my baby
We're not in Alexandra Township
The singing you hear
Is not of Zionists
It is a song of joy

    'Why are we sleeping in the open, mama?'

Father Ntintili pushed us out
For a new tenant
Ready to pay new rental
Obedient as a servant.

    'I am frightened, mama.'

Don't be frightened, my child,
Papa has a baboon
Nobody dare bewitch you
In the Kalahari your father
Travelled by baboon
The Masarwa has deadly mutis

    'I want to see papa's baboon.'

Not tonight, my child,
Papa keeps it somewhere
Unseen by the naked eye
Eye of a child.

JUKSKEI GHOST

Be calm
Nobody dare unearth you
The searchlights you see
Are men's fears
On those who have passed death
Closeted in their apartment
Waiting for the day of resurrection.

Upon the Jukskei River bank
You've friends
Praying for your soul
That you may rest
In God's kingdom
Till eternity.

They've chosen you as neighbour
Rather than submit
To exploitation.

I ventured to pacify you
Be calm
Very soon it will be over.

ALEXANDRA TOWNSHIP

Alexandra Township, you were my home
Thirty years ago.
From Vasco Da Gama to London Lane
Prowling your streets at will
Mindless of your dangers
Mindless of your darkness
Mindless of your hooligans.

You had fine management
Black and white, managing you amicably
Never was there stinking in your street.

Now you're left uncared for
You're heap of rubbish
You're company of debris
Your buildings are dilapidated
Isn't someone in charge?

A WORKER'S LAMENT

From five in the morning,
My lean body is crushed against the jostling crowd,
For pittance, I make my way among the passengers,
Swaying coaches make my heart to jerk in fear,
That I may not my little ones see any more
Yet for food and rent I must work.

'SEBENZA'. The whole day long;
The foreman and the Induna scream
They should because the boss explained: 'productivity'.
Pale lips; hunger exposes my empty stomach,
Starch water only my stomach has breakfasted.
Hunger takes away pride from a man's self-respect
But the burning heart for revenge vows:
'Kahle, a day will come; me boss, you boy.'

The listless sun leaves to the night,
To blanket the light
Thousands of pattering feet homeward drag
And leave the Shops to the watchmen.
Again I join the jostling crowd,
Fifteen miles homeward journey to travel,
Crammed like Jeppe Station victims,
I stand on a bench to save myself
Being crushed to death.

FRIDAY NIGHT IN GHANA

South of the Sahara is Ghana
The only country
To get freedom
South of the Sahara.

South of the Sahara
Its government decided
To grant its indigenous people
                Freedom.

South of the Sahara
The world family decided
To tighten its sanctions
For human rights.

South of the Sahara
Seriously considered lifting liquor laws
To off-set economic sanctions.

In Ghana the people flocked
On Friday night
To consider the main issue.
In a stampede for the taste of beer
They forgot the main issue:
                PASS-LAWS.

MARKET SQUARE

We gathered on that rainy day
On Market Square
Thousands of us, black faces
On Human Rights Day
Declared in a court of law
By the United Nations
Against inhumanity.

Thousands of us, black faces
On Market Square
Human Rights Day
In thunderous voice
    'Freedom in our lifetime.'

Thousands of us, black faces
On that summer day
On Market Square
Shook the world
    'Votes for all.'

As in Africa
Gathered on this day
On Freedom Square, celebrating Uhuru
Here too, deep south
On Market Square
    'Mayibuye.'

Thousands of voices shook the world
Length and breadth
North, south, east, west,
    'Uhuru, kwacha, pula, mayibuye.'
In our lifetime.

UNDYING CULTURE

Heaped in mine dumps
Is undying culture
Born and bred in Africa
Traditionally recorded.

Down south from the Congo Basin
Is blended
Be it beating of drums
Feet stamping
Gumbooting
Is Africa.

Three hundred years
It defied onslaught
In white garment
Blue striped
Cross and stars
'Bayete hallelujah.'

Singing, singing everywhere
'Ngisebenzela abantwana bami
Ngibathengela ibhayi elisha
Bhayi lami, bhayi lami.'

A CITY WITHIN A CITY

South of a city is a city.
Ten miles south of a city
Founded fifty years ago
By the by-laws of a city
Under Ordinance 10 of a province
        Up north.

It was not a choice of their own
Thousands of souls live south of a city
Out of reach
South of a city
Foot, cycle south of a city.

Is begun by fireside
On a.camp
A yellowish rock on a surface
        Dazzled
        'A thousand gilt
        Worth this rock.'

Thousands flocked to this camp
In search of a rock —
For wealth to command the world
North, south, east and west,
Scampering for labour.
        'Wozani madoda.'

Thousands flocked to this camp
To dig, dig, through the surface of the earth
Side by side
The diggers lived
Undisturbed by colour.

By the declaration of an ordinance
By the stroke of a pen
Slum clearance was promulgated.
Silent protest. Soundless murmurings
Moved thousands of souls
South of a city.

A million souls, south of the city,
Bursting seams
South of the city refluxed
    'Are you Xhosa, Zulu, Tswana?'
    'I don't know.'
    'You must decide on citizenship.'
    'African!'
    'Stateless!'

WEEP NOT SOPHIATOWN

Politics can be cruel
Can bury someone alive
Silenced and gagged
Amidst the din of protest.

Peacefully you lived with your neighbour
Not a grouse from either side
Artificially separated
Minus your neighbour's affairs.

Someone climbed on an ox-wagon
Fresh from the country
In haranguing speeches
Agitated your removal.

Time and again napping
In the Houses of Parliament
'Hoor, hoor, Triomf.'
A vain victory.

Your memory of Toby street house
M.D., C.H.B., L.R.C.P., M.R.C.P.,
Not a plain sailing.
Triomf eye wash.

You're still Sophiatown
Remembered in Yearly Book
Anno Domini
Nineteen hundred and ten.

THESE BLACK HANDS

Down in the bowels
Of the earth;
I've extracted wealth
That gives you comfort.

I've toiled hard
Complaining very little
Drilled rock
Sunk shafts,
Picked and shovelled
I am now obsolete
And useless.

My white brother
Has denied me
The right to defend myself
Turned me into his serf
   'No kaffir trade union.'

The bosses have combined:
Formed a chamber,
Recruitment of 'native' labour
Fixing of wages
And regulating it.

I am now useless
And obsolete
Suffering from lung disease
Coughing blood
And short of breath.

COUNTER 14

Around Albert Street
Are faces pale, haggard and desperate
Lips cracked from cavity
Scrambling over job-seeking

In a yard
Twenty feet high
Bounded from sightseeing
        many more
Seated, shifting, yawning

Not even a bazaar
Would have so many customers
Queueing
Their fate
On a white face

'Escort'
72 hours grace
Out of urban area
To starve, rob, steal
In own homeland.

A MAN'S GRAVE IS BY THE WAYSIDE

The villagers thought
They were affronting you
By refusing you a decent
Burial spot.
They buried you in this thicket
By the wayside
Out of sight.

You're facing north
Lebowa la kgomo
Thought to be your home
Whence you came
To this village
Unaccepted.

You're occupying an undisturbed spot
By the wayside
Free from arrivals
Arguing who is the first arrival
To this thicket
Out of sight.

You're fulfilling the historical adage
    'Lebitla la monna le tseleng.'
Undisturbed in your thicket
Out of sight.

Someone is taking note of you
On badimo day
She poses by your graveside
In the thicket.

Solemnly she poses

On badimo day
In meditation
In this thicket
Out of sight.

IRRESOLUTE

Elsewhere
My way of life is being decided
To fit into a modern pattern
A pattern of how I should govern
In the world of today
How nations have made strides
Their own destiny.

I've been too long shackled
Imprisoned soul and mind
Shackled to protest
Even at asking for living wage
In big and small towns
At every corner of a street.

I've been imprisoned
Feet and hands
To march in protest
To Adderley Street.

Now I am an irresolute creature
Pensioned here
With no knowledge
A citadel of sound governmentship.

BORDER INDUSTRY I

Pack up
Your stock and machinery
Homeland labour
Is cheap
No industrial agreement
No trade union organisation
No agitators

You are assured
Of output
Best Quality
World Competitive
As long as you
Don't label it
'HOMELAND'.

BORDER INDUSTRY II

You should be grateful
I came here for your benefit
For your family's sake
To be with you daily.

You would be worse starving
Had I not moved
Stock and barrel
From the riches of city life
To this barren land
     Devoid of culture.

You're better off
Than your city brother
Crushed into overcrowdedness
Throttled by rental
     Owning nothing.

You lord over your plot
Raising mealies, pumpkins
Owning a goat for milk.

Keep your head clear
You've no reason
To complain of underpayment
Keep away from destructive talks
     About how I
Have come to exploit you.

WEALTH FOR FEW

You slice into a portion of my field
Without asking me.
You dig minerals
Out of my field
Without a word
Do you regard me as a mute?

            You said
I am redundant
After using me for years.
            You said
I am useless
After draining all my strength.

            Now
You follow me
Right into my homeland.

KEEP AWAY FROM POLITICS

I am a young state
Beginning to crawl
If you talk politics
You'll upset my plans
Keep away from politics.

My neighbour has promised
A lump sum
If only I keep you away
From politics.

I've called on industrialists
Sent an emissary abroad
Recruiting technicians
Don't upset my plans.

Meanwhile
I've untrained agriculturists
Third-grade teachers
Make use of them.

Build your children schools
Give wholeheartedly
Till your land
Keep away from politics.

IN HIS MASTER'S FOOTSTEPS

I
A monkey emblem on a wall
   Signifying a tribe —
A drunken clerk strolls
About the office building
Buffing foul language
As a clerk behaves.

The office is the pride of the tribe
Since the Bantu Authority enactment.
The pride of the tribe
Justice carried out
The chief a rubber stamp.

An artistic painting inside —
Rose petal; green and yellow painted
Artistic work of a student
Progress since Bantu Education.

On the stoep
Patiently waits a permit seeker
Retired to the homeland
By grace of old age.

'Are you born in this village?'
'Sixty-five years ago.'
'Do you know the old settlement?'
'Before your father was born.'
'Your reference is foreign?'
'I am internationalist.'
'You speak English?'
'A linguist.'
'You're impossible.'

'Send me to the chief.'

II
Have you decided to return home?'
  'Refluxed.'
'You owe hut-tax?'
'Paid in rental.'
'Not reflected in our record?'
'In the city treasury.'
'It must be recovered.'
  'Irrecoverable.'
'Damned to deal with a vagabond.
Report within twenty one days
With fifty rand.'

III
'What a cheek!
Fifty rand refund!
Not in my life
A note like this
From a native chief.'
  'Illiterate.'
'Seventy-two hours of grace
Back to homeland.'

NOT FOR MY LIKING

You're observant
Conscientious
Responsible
Are you an aide
In finance?
     'When not involved.'

Independence has had us
Autonomous government
Manage our affairs
Raise funds
Are you capable of secretaryship?
     'Capable.'

You receive money
You forge duplicates
I collect money
Do you mind?
     'Full responsibility. Nothing less.'

UNDEFENDED CASE

I
Your client should have told you
That white man's law don't work
In our court of law
Defending criminals.

Our procedure is free participation —
Consensus arrived at
Is binding
On a chief
To pronounce sentence.

II
Order him in
Severely shall he be dealt with —
Bringing a white man here.
Severely. He shall pay heavily.

Your wealth
        Cattle, goats, sheep
Would have been your penalty
Were you not poor.
        BANISHMENT
Shall serve you right.

TIME

Time is not always money
Time is Administration,
Coming in time,
     Queueing
     Offering bribes
     Reaching a counter
     Documents stamped
That is time
Not always money
But patience.

WRETCHEDNESS

Look, brother,
How wretched you look
Pinned to the past
Cattle your status in wealth
Counting them on your fingers.

You're now watching them
Emaciated
Worthless for stewing
Stumbling daily on death

The land is solid substance
Gusting wind
Sweeping dust
Wind as hot as breath
No sign of rain.

Yet you still pin your hope
On the past
When grazing ground
Was as vast as the endless world
Each season pasturing there.

Look, brother,
Arid patches of land
Dry parched land
Barren.

Brother, take a little stroll
Out of sight
Tremendous changes you'll have
Suitable here and there.

Brained in your skull
Tremendous amount
Capable of plucking off
Wretchedness.

Life is not intended to be perpetual
uTixo uhamba nge rei
Rich to-day, poor tomorrow
Maybe tomorrow is your neighbour
uTixo uhamba nge rei.

ESTRANGED

My good lord, I am an only one
Without an organisation
A workers' organisation, a trade union
    'What!'

I am alienated from a country
I built for three hundred years
Roads, bridges, mines, factories
These calloused hands built
I'm now estranged in an undeveloped area
    'Be explicit!'

I accepted independence
Free from restriction, pass-laws, discrimination
Appropriated to make my own laws
    'I said keep away from politics!'

Your lordship, it is not politics
It is bread and butter talk
A daily talk in factories
In buses and lunch hour talk
    'A commission of inquiry is in the offing.'

Thank you, my lord,
I do hope it does not recommend
Yellow union
    'What! Yellow union
    What is that?'

My fears, your lordship,
Are based on what I see:
Class-interest
    'Class-interest?

Blacks are a classless society.'

My new-born country
Has Chamber of Commerce
National bank
Farmers' society
Is that not class society?
(Aside): 'I'll have him locked up.'

DEMARCATION LINE

A demarcation line
Runs on my doorstep
Leaving no space to stretch
And a little across
Is my neighbour
Relied on me
For labour and friendliness.

Side by side we've lived
In good-neighbourly friendship
Relying on each other
For labour and friendliness

Now an artificial line
Demands a passport
Each time I stretch
Across the line
When visiting my neighbour.

My neighbour
Tells me
He does not mind
Sliced into me.

AN IDIOT

I'd thought this boy
Is an idiot
Obedient and docile
A ja-baas boy
    'Wat sê jy, Meneer Wilson?'

Meneer, I'd thought this boy
A fool, a stupid idiot
And imbecile, three hundred years
Deceiving myself
    'Hoe het jy nou gesien?'

Meneer,
My binoculars are penetrative
Deep into the mind
    'Wat het jy gesien?'

Too terrifying to tell
Incredible
Drive us into the sea.
    'Wat?'

Believe it or not
With assegais
Into the sea
    'Dit sal die dag wees.'

SINS OF THE PARENTS

Don't blame me
You accepted inferior education
In the face of protests and anger
    'A piece of bread,' you said,
    'Is better than nothing.'

You ordered me out of your home
    'A piece of bread is better than nothing.'
Your word was
As 'right-about-turn'.

'Your certificate is not worth
    Toilet paper.'
This day
I failed the aptitude test.

Your very benefactor says:
I am not competent in
Filling in a census form
    'A piece of bread is better than nothing.'
You said.

I am like an idiot
Trying to fit myself
Into a society of intellectuals
Pushed by you into this position
Your 'piece of bread' is shit.

THE NAME 'BOY'

You do not care
When you hurt me
Slip of tongue
Sucked from childhood.

You're now a man
Knowing it's hurting
To call someone by a demeaning name
Yet in spite of your knowing
You still call me 'boy'.

My tolerance is running out
Angry fluid is saturating
Full of venom.

HANGING SERVITUDE

Mastership and baaskap are stained
Stained into the mind and soul
Since the day of conquest
Till nowadays —
Hard to erase.

It's not a slip of tongue
To every white face
        'Baas, Master, Missus, Nooi.'
Stained into the mind.

Someone is trying to erase the stain
By tip of nib
By piecemeal concessions

And elsewhere someone
By redivision of land
Into black and white blocks

But hard to erase
Baaskapism.
Stained in blood streams
Since the day of conquest

Hard to accept
In heart-tearing veins
A gushing stream of resentment.

TRIBALISM IN ACTION

I am seeing it done in the open
By an indigenous tribe
Upon misfortunates
Misfortunated by Bantu labour tenancy.
    Cast into oblivion.

I am seeing it practised
In the open:
In kgotlas, finance, schools,
Ignoring feelings of misfortunates.

I am hearing it by tlhokwa-la-tsela
That Utholeng have no say
Cursed to remain mute
    Dumb as setlotlwane.

    Wait brother!
A day will come
A day the world will come to reason
No more traditions.

A LEAN YEAR

It was toward sunset
The sun dipping into the horizon
Glowingly reddish
As if scorching the rims
We returning from the fields
Women preparing evening meals
And boys milking.

From where the sun had travelled
In the morning
Intermingled in the wind
As if of storm
Were of speckling objects
Racing to the setting sun.

    'Ka Morena!
    Are we engulfed
    Between fire and hurricane?'

The sun touched the horizon
Glowingly red
Moulding into sulphur
Brimstone flame
And gradually threw us into darkness.

Darkness was gradually
Dimming light,
Leaving us into complete darkness
Between darkness and hurricane
Of flying objects
Now settled unseen.

We were crept into fear

The brimstone fire
The hurricane objects
Envelop us.

By dusk
By fowls awakening
Throughout the village
Young and old
Rushed out of dwellings
    'Belebele tsieng,'
Was echoed throughout the village.

For joy and sorrow
We scooped containers full
Unmindful of reptiles
A hearty relishing meal
Untasted for a long time.

The earth warmed
And dripped off
As if in command
The locusts began rising up
Into the breezy wind
Leaving the ground
As desolate as if nothing
Had ever vegetated it.

The sky was again like moulding smoke
Becoming thick
Devastating any hope of rainfall
Westward blowing
Carrying belebele tsieng.

In bewilderment and joy
For relishing meal and bare land

A rejoicing period now
A bleak future
Our livestock added sorrow
To joy.

No tint of grass was left
Stalk mealies were stalky
Stalky to marrow
A scorched earth.

Our previous year crops
Were decreasing
We shared
Lived much closer
Until nothing was left.

We begged
Where there was smoke,
We begged
A morsel to sustain us.

Nature is kind
It teaches unknowns
Hidden knowledge
Discovered by suffering
We survived on motlopi.

WASTING AWAY

Two thousand Souls
Lived on hopeless hope
A vacuum hope
Soundless and unhearing
Each day as yesterday
No fain of hope.

Long days, long nights
Dreary as every night and day
Unfeelingly, nonchalant
Unmoved as there in firmament
Unmoved even by the day of the birth of Christ
Soulless.

Was unmoving in that world
Undisturbed by outside world
Spiritless.

Lived the thousand Souls
In the unmoved world
Hope against doom
Each day as yesterday.

ON A HILLTOP
(Dedicated to Nicodemus Maloka Moloele)

On a hilltop is a man
On a hilltop in a village
Dwells an old man
As old as the last generation
Yet his memory is fresh as yesterday
Fresher than yours and mine.

From the hilltop
His memory descends on daily happenings
Happened ninety years ago
As fresh as daily news
'Springbok flats,' quoth he,
'Is a British Colony.
Springboks were as many as those herds.
Never a day was I without meat.'

From Springbok flats strides he
Proud hilltop man
Unto the estate, of a statesman
A general
Bestowed premiership
Of the Union of South Africa
A cook, gardener, handyman?

Honest, faithful, diligent
A locomotive; peak-capped
On a way to Markstraat
Through Kerkstraat
Seated behind General Eiselen
Proud young man
A transfer
In the service of the Stadsraad.

Proud old man is he now
'Wait, I am still talking.
I was given over to General Eiselen.
He taught me driving
I was the first black to drive
Others were Cape Coloured.'

Proud young man was he
Unlettered, yet understood
Road Signs
White gloved policeman
Old Smithy by-crossing signs.
Stop — staan. Halt. Verby.
'Bravo boy, you've passed driving
Splendid, kaffir. Brain of a whiteman.'

Proud young man
In land of Malays, Hottentots, Bushmen
Proud young man from the bushveld
Sweltering weather, hot as the tropics
Drove through Adderley Street
To the Houses of Parliament
Proud brown face never flickering
As ebony as mahogany.
Drove the general and his wife.

BRING DIE KOFFIE

Môre oggend bring my die koffie
In ouma se koppie
Moenie die deur hard klop nie
Ouma slaap tot laat
Bring die koffie.

As ek môre siek wees
Roep die dokter,
Wit dokter
Nie kaffir dokter nie.
Ek wil nie kaffir medisyne nie
Wit medisyne wil ek hê.

As ek dood is
Moenie die badimo bedank nie
Ek is nie kaffir nie
Ek is witman
Bring my die koffie.

Begraaf my nie in die beeste kraal nie
Begraaf my in die kerkjaart
Roep die predikant, wit moruti
Nie kaffir moruti
Laat my die nagmaal drink.

Piet, as ek dood is
Pas op die nooi
Slaap in die voorkamer
Moenie die deur oop maak nie
As iemand klop
Maak net oop as ek klop
Goeie naand Piet.

GRAVE OF UNKNOWN WHITEMAN

Rest in peace, old man
A heap of rocks on your grave
Is a token of respect
Bestowed on you.

You chose this part of the country
For a home
On a slope of those rocks
Was your community
And across that road
You sowed corn
And watered your cattle in that pan.

In years of dearth
We shared together
Helped each other in time of need.

Rest in peace, old man
Your kindred are here
Paying due respect
Rest in peace!

MAN-MADE LIGHTNING

I hear stories! Incredible stories
Told around beer vessel
In the lapas
By shrivelled old-timers
By rheumatic grannies.

'Tladi-mothwana has struck'
She assents
'My neighbour's home
It went through every corner
Helped itself to meal.'

'Morena!' affirms another
'I saw it with my own two eyes
Cooking a chicken
Stomaching it piecemeal.'

'My bones never tell lies
They fell twaaga-dima'
Says a reputed doctor
Somewhere in the village.

'It is still smoking
I smell the pervading smell
Of twaaga-dima
The struck home must be cleansed.

'Rain shall fall this year
Thunder, storm, Kganyapa
Will rain ruin
Unless the affected home is cleansed.'

I swear by mother's name

The Apostles cleansed the home
Plastering blue-white crosses
Calling upon hallelujah!

TEN WITCHES

A monotonous lone beating drum
Menacing sound
In the darkness
Moonless night
At cockcrow.

On a nearby tree
Ominous shadow
A nocturnal summons
To the witches to assemble
Heart-tearing sound
      Death.

In the shadow of a bushy tree
Hummed ten witches
Men and women
Naked
Discussing revenge

Revengeful: 'bing, bing'
Near, nearer sounds in sleep
Peacefully sleeping
In dreamland.

Then itches she
Twists her naked body
As if coiling into a snake
Thud. She slumbers.

II
Like log-lump
Pale lips
Tongue tight

Protruding eye-balls
Is she
Five days ago healthy.

'A mystery sickness,' says a white doctor.
'Boloi,' replies her mother,
'She's dying.'
He feels her pulse. Shakes his head.
'Rigor mortis? Nil.
Mysterious sickness,' he says in breath.

In a motionless world
Lies she
Morbid
Life in death
Lies she in a motionless world.

'Bing, bing, bing.'
Disturbing the night,
Monotonous, lone beating sound
To her burial place
This morning, lies she.

'Bing, bing, bing.'
Rises a coffin
Surfaced
'Cut her tongue.'

ASSEBLIEF BAAS
a farm labour tenant

'More kom'. You've said, baas
Before cockcrow
I must be up
Plaas kom

I know, baas
If I fail
Ten lashes on my back
Ten lashes and trek pas

Asseblief, baas
My child is sick
Sick from bewitching
The kaffir doctor say so
Bones never lie
The white doctor know nothing

By night
Hy slaap nie, baas
Hy sien die spook
Die wit nooi
In die groot bonnet.

Ek vra, baas
A day off
To consult my spirits
A white goat slaughter

Dankie, baas
Die picannin is up
Blood picannin drink
The kaffir doctor right

The white doctor
Know nothing.

EPISODES IN THE RURAL AREAS

I

'Baas I want to get married.'

'What do you want me to do for you?'

'To help me with eight head of cattle.'

'How will you pay back?'

'I shall work for you until I have recovered their price.'

'Alright Jan, I shall advance you eight cattle. Piet will play father for you. Piet see that you get me a receipt. Nothing else must be written on the receipt except eight head of cattle.'

Piet heads the bogadi to Jan's parents-in-law. Mary, Jan's bride, accompanies him. She's immediately engaged for domestic chores. Jan is on out-door duties. During the day Captain Smythe has sexual intercourse with Mary. Jan is told by others who had noticed the boss's misdeeds. Jan deserts the farm in the evening with his wife. Capt Smythe reports him to the district magistrate. He appears in court for desertion. He is asked to plead.

'Mokolo sleeps with my wife.'

The magistrate is astounded.

'What!'

'Yes baas, Mokolo sleeps with my wife.'

'Did you not promise to work for him until you've recovered the price of eight head of cattle you paid for bogadi?'

'Yes, but he sleeps with my wife.' The magistrate remained adamant.

'You must go back and work for him.'

'Haaikona baas, he sleeps with my wife.'

II

On a farm in Rust De Winter are squatters working on option for a farmer. Mr. Mackay has a son primed for farming duties. The only children nearby are squatters' ones.

Mr. Mackay plays with them. On a certain day one of the squatters obediently greets Mr. Mackay.

'Baas, I want to talk to you.'

'What is it about, Piet?'

'Young baas has spoilt my daughter.'

'What! My son spoilt your daughter? Do you mean he has got your daughter pregnant?'

'Yes, baas. She is in her third month. She says the young baas got her like that.'

'Look, Piet. Your kaffir children have been coming here. Do you think a bull will leave a bitch if it exposes itself. It is your daughter that has spoilt my son. Get out of this place.'

III

'Hans, my ox has disappeared. Do you perhaps know who has stolen it?'

'No, baas.'

'Have you perhaps sold it as yours by mistake?'

'I sold no ox, baas.'

'What about the one slaughtered for your niece's wedding?'

'I have not been to the wedding.'

'You're a bad uncle not to attend your niece's wedding.'

Hans remains silent.

'I am attending the wedding this afternoon. Will you come with me?'

Hans drops his head.

Mr. Post leaves without Hans. He squats at a beer-

drinking group. He asks to see the skin of the slaught-
ered beast.
'I buy skins,' he tells the father of the home.
'The skin is for the uncle of my daughter,' he is
reminded.
'Alright, I will take it home for him.'
Mr. Post has it loaded on a horse-cart.
'Hans' he calls out, 'I've brought your skin. Come
and see it.'
'Hans comes, his hands folded; avoiding to look at the
skin.
'Hans don't worry. I won't call the police for you. Go
and fetch sixteen of your oxen. I shall choose one to
replace mine.'
The sixteen oxen are driven to Mr Post.
'Alright Hans. Thank you. All these sixteen replace
mine. You and I are old friends. We don't want police
intervention.'

IV
Geelbooi and Thomas arrive on a farm late in the
afternoon. Thomas is neatly dressed. He looks sophis-
ticated. He seems to be following the farmer as he tells
Geelbooi that the sale of livestock is tomorrow. Geel-
booi now and then nods foolishly. 'Yaa, baas, yaa,
baas,' he keeps on repeating.
The trouble comes when the farmer asks: 'Waar vanaf
kom julle?'
'Skilpadfontein,' replies Thomas.
'Wat! Nie 'Skilpadfontein baas' nie?'
Geelbooi is shown a hut for night shelter.
'Maar nie vir daardie Engelse kaffir nie.'

V
Thomas has not yet received a lesson that this is the

Platteland.

'Kaffirs' are not allowed just to speak without respect to a white person. He enters a novelty shop and examines authors' names on the books.

'Hoekom vra jy nie wat jy soek nie?'

'Sorry, madam. I have already found one that I want.'

'Ja! Jy praat nog Engels.'

'A bit of Afrikaans, too, nooi.'

'Wat is jy?'

'An author.'

The shopowner changes to English.

'I would like to see what you've written.'

A month later Thomas arrives with the book he has written.

'Can I have it for reading?'

The next following month, Thomas calls again.

'Your book is down-to-earth. You should add to what happened in the later life of your heroine. She is such a marvellous girl to have braved shame by not discarding her baby.'

A WIDOWER

The impurities in your blood
Are impurities
Associated in your deceased wife
You're to be purified
In compounded herbs.

You're widowed
Now untouchable
Confined indoors
For a full seasonal year.

You're impure in all dealings
     Social gatherings
     Sexual intercourse
And in food sharing.
Separate dishes are reserved for you.

Never leave home before sunrise
Never arrive after sunset
Don't think of remarrying.

WEEP NOT

Weep not, brother,
Fifteen years you've seen her dying
Unable to play her role
As a woman
Fifteen years sick abed.

Are you now willy-nillying
In compounded herbs restored
No existing impurities
Fifteen years in purity?

Custom is tradition
A human sickness
Intolerable in this height
Sunset to sunrise cloistered
In quarantine.

THIS DAMNED LIFE

It should be too tantalizing
Unbearable, heartbreaking
To contemplate this life
Forsaking your child
Because your mother
Will say: 'I don't like her.'

How many have you
Forsaken since yesterday?
In bewilderment, fear
    'I don't like her.'

You count your fingers
Each a child
Forsaken, unborn
    'I don't like her.'

In that pot-belly is your germination
Unborn baby
Reeling in that pot-belly
Are you it, too,
Going to forsake?
Damn your mother's adamant
    'I don't like her.'

UNDECAYING OLD TREE

You are a witch
Old triple-trunked
Spineless and immobile
Withered and dry
And numbed.
Your days are long numbered.

You are an old hag
Terrifying hag
Shadowless
Immobile as your branches
You should long be axed.

Sodom Gomorrah!
Is that your name?
Unbemoaned.

A DOG FINDS A GOOD HOME I

I was an only girl
Of the four boys
Born on a Friday
Last born of my mother's children.

By the time I was born
My mother was dry of milk
I had a touch of malnutrition
And was emaciated

By chance a traveller
Heard me crying
Asked my mother
Offered me an orphanage home.

The first night
I spent on a cosy bed
For breakfast
I breakfasted on dogmor gravy.

Within a week
I was robust
Began barking
Chasing goats
And am now
A sentry.

A DOG FINDS A GOOD HOME II

I was only a girl
Of four boys
And I was last to be born.
My mother was dry
Of milk when I was born.

My mother had five husbands
Each visiting her in turns
I got to know my father
On a Friday night.
He licked me
And left me a bone.

I got emaciated
For I was not strong
To reach my mother's teats.
Often I sucked after my brothers
Had had all the milk.

I was sold to a traveller
O! how I cried
Snatched from my mother and brothers.
My heart was like bursting
And I nearly fell into a pit.

The first night in my new home
I spent at the foot
Of my master's bedding.
A first time to sleep in warmth.
In the morning,
I breakfasted on tea and dogmor.

I still pined to see

My mother and brothers.
I tried to skip a fence
I fell back
And hurt my spine
My master applied elasto
On my backbone
The pain soon vanished.

Within a week
I could bark and chase goats
And am now
A love of the home.

MANNERS

I have seen a bitch
A well-mannered bitch
Better than its name
Refusing a bull-terrier, a hound
      Love-making.

Night long it refused
Snarling
A bull-terrier and hound
Tearing each other's skin.

At dawn
A nondescript terrier arrived
By-passing the bleeding bull and hound
Undisturbed.

She
In lady-like style
Followed the terrier
And interlocked.

A LONELY OLD WOMAN

Once upon a time there lived an old woman
She was very poor
She lived in a house without a door
Her companion was a pig.

One day she went out
Into the forest
To gather faggots of wood
She left the pig
In charge
The pig ate all the meal
And died from overeating.

The poor old woman
Was left without a companion.
Every night she sat musing
For she was very lonely.

'Piggy, piggy,'
She sang
'Wake up.
The food you ate
Was for supper.'

The pig woke up
And assured the old woman
She would never steal again.

A NIGHT HAWK

Straddled on ding-tong bell bicycle
Is a blue-nine
A Blue-sky jail-breaker
On Harley-Davidson handlebars
    Reed-swaying.

On shiny bicycle
Ding-tong bells
Reed-swaying
To lavish on my sister's earnings
This ragamuffin
Blue-sky five-star prisoner.

A Blue-sky blue-nine
Unreformed parole
Reed-swaying on dong-tong bicycle
    Reconnoitring.

Five-star Blue-sky blue-nine
Unrepented criminal
Undeterred
Skips over the fence.

A night hawk
Experienced burglar
No second to waste
Thins into the night.

'Morena!
What is this?'
A five-star Blue-sky blue-nine
Passionately moved
By baby in arms

Retraces his way
    'I am sorry, madam.'

KHOIKHOI-SON-OF-MAN

I thought I was soul and skin
Pedigree muntu
Until yesterday I heard the truth
Grandfather was a Khoisan.

A slave of a trekboer
Fleeing from the Cape laws
Freeing slaves.

At night
He was tied to an oxwagon wheel
Groaning
Day by day leading sixteen span
Fleeing from the Cape.

Night by night
Somewhere there was a cock-crow
A barking dog
A smell of damp fuel
Then he realized that beyond that ridge
Could be a village
Of people like him.

He unfastened himself,
Trotted out of the camp,
Vanished into the night.

At dawn he was at a village
Begging to be taken into the tribe
   'A tribesman, hunter chief's servant and messen-
                                                    ger.'

Swift as an antelope was he
Outstripping runners

Chased by dogs.
   'Ka modimo,' they swore.
   'He is a man of the cloud.
   Ompone ke tswa kae?'
A legendary tale: where have you seen me?
   'I have seen you from the cloud.'
Khoikhoi-Son-of-Man.

I know since yesterday
that he was my grandfather
Khoikhoi-Son-of-Man.

SHAMEFUL LEGACY

Had I known the speed of years
I would have retreated into my mother's womb
Safely snug into her womb
Fifty years safely snugged.

I would have been safe
Against powerful forces
Sweeping across natural boundaries
In search of human wealth,
Gold and pearl, land and human assets
Safely snugged into my mother's womb.

I would have studied the art of politics
Undisturbed in my mother's womb.
    'A powerful man talks less
    By barrel of a gun.'

Now years have ebbed me
From marrow to toe,
Leaving an unwanted legacy
Of poverty, humiliation, oppression,
To be inscribed on my tomb stone.

BLAME YOURSELF

Time and again
I checked myself
Doubting your sincerity
Suspecting you of double-crossing
As a chameleon passing through green grass.

I loathe to throw too much dust into your face
But allow me to say a little
You were unfaithful, insincere, unreliable
But still I hung on you.

I expressed my love by singing
Suffice it to remind you of this song!
    'You play a game of pretending
    But you'll be sorry some day
    Here's my love the last glowing ember
    Give the kiss that I shall remember
    Days I've left you.'

I was a fool then not to leave
I tailed after you like an idiot
I thought you were a virgin
Untouched since your mother's womb
Fresh as a ripening apple.

You displayed your fine colours
The day I vowed I'll work for you
You were unco-operative
You turned hell in the sunshine
Pray, let sleeping dogs lie low.

I was a confounded fool
Unheeding admonitions

Grandfather's finger bent like a sickle
Severing the relationship
Cloudy dreams like the smoke of damp fuel.

Utter no word of cursing
Brood not over your misery
Don't blame me.
Blame yourself.

SCALPEL

Thirty-four of us lay sick
In Ward Thirty-four
Trembling at the thought of scalpel.

    'Porter.'
Thus my fate is nearer —
On the porter's wheeled-cart
To the scalpel house.

'Have you children?'
    I don't know.
'How many are they?'
    I've forgotten.

UNFINISHED MANUSCRIPT

Quick
You've only a few hours left
To finish your manuscript
Death is waiting at the door
Impatient to pounce upon you
At any moment.

You're assigned to complete
This version!
Arrival of bride seeking
Unclear.

If you fail
You'll have failed scores
Reading your manuscript
    'A flop'
They will curse
    'A flop.'

By the gate
Awaits an ambulance
To convey you to a place
Of no return
A Scalpel House
With the merciless knife.

Make haste
Roll up your manuscript
Death is at the door
    Impatient.

A VISIT TO ANGLE ROAD

I visited your surroundings
The other day
I was struck by the deplorable state
Bhana's shop is in;
Corroding iron sheets, peeling walls, broken windows
The front door is missing
I am told the shop is a refuge
For hobos, prostitutes, drunkards
And the dregs of life.

The purpose of my visit
Was to see all:
The Bhana shop yard
Is turned into a warehouse
I could hardly make out
A passage leading out to your left
Piles of cases, boxes were piled to the roof-top.

I turned back
Through the yard
To my surprise no vestige of rooms remained
Only a single corridorless hall
I could breathe passing through it.

It was marvellous to see you
In new outlook
Your floor is well tarred
The air is purified
I hope you're relieved from water cart spray.

Money is a sin
Zulu Congregational Church is turned
Into a workshop

The vestry is a sleeping porch
What a smell in the vestry!

I should have known
You prohibited entry
Into your left angle
You were perturbed by CNA newspaper sellers
Fighting, gambling, whores
Were intolerable.
I can see your reason
In asking for the CNA back gate to be shut.

I really wanted to see everything
I expected a forest of gum trees
Along the railway line from Jeppe to Doornfontein,
Macfarlane, Thornton Transport Contractors
And British Cables,
What happened to all these?

LEARNING

Learning has no limitations
Last year I made mistakes
The previous year I blundered
This year, I shall do better.

In the Garden of Eden
I learned to make fire
Clothe myself
And have children.

The world is boundless
Each one of us
Can contribute
    Provided
We pluck off
Complexes, fear and mistrust.

OP DIE STOEP

Sit 'n engelse Kaffir
Op die stoep
En lees 'n papier
Engelse Koerant
Vas diep in.

Rond die stoep
Draai 'an, draai 'an die witman
Die wit baas
N' kyk aan die Kaffir
Engelse Kaffir
Wat engelse koerant lees.

'Die wêreld is omgedraai
Kaffirs lees koerante
Hul is gemors.'
Sê die wit baas.

'Wat sê die papier?'
      'Ek lees nog!'
Antwoord die engelse Kaffir
Diep in, in die papier.

Rooi word die wit baas
      'Ek wens al die kaffirs
      Moet toegesluit word
      Hul is almal kommuniste.'

LOVE IN ABEYANCE

I expressed my love
When you and I were still young
'Wait,' you said
'I am still young.'

Life is a long journey
East and west it travels
South and north it transects
Daily taking toll on us
East you went
West I took.

In those long years
I pined to meet you
I languished in the hope
Of meeting you some day
Where east and west meet.

I sought you in Suburbs
        Parktown North
        Craighall Park
        Lower Houghton.
Not a sight of you.

I heard you were lying sick abed
Pining to see me
Each breath a voice
Each footstep and knock
                Anon.

Death has no abeyance
It's swift
It snatches.

Anna, my stay here
Is not long.
I've made preparations.
Very soon, you and I
In God's Heaven
Shall swing arms.
STAY WELL.

ALONE IN THE VAST SEA

Though my friends curse me a traitor
Here I lie in this vast sea
Watched by the stars and moon
Blue enthral, heavenly stars
Watching over me, over the night,
Pitying my fate
Dumped into this vast sea
Like leprosy inflicting others
Who may follow my cause.

The wind outside is stormy and furious
Cursing my presence, uncalled-for presence
Wrecking wind of hail storm
In this vast sea
Unsailed since mortar and scaffold
Ripped off every vestige of vegetation.

The sea has warmth
Eiderdowned with blue layers
Smoothing, sailing eiderdown
Yet unwetting
Roofed over by enthral stars
Sparkling in heaven
I entombed between sea and stars
Crying mercy of the sea
Vouchsafe till morn.

By my side she lies
Uncomplainingly complaining of my traitorship
Vowed on a day
Till death shall part us.

Bright morning is on this sea
Rolling back the skies

For warmth and beauty
Musical morning, unheard elsewhere
Welcoming the mortar man
Satisfied of my safety
    'Good morning,' says he
    'Good morning, my lord.'